W9-ATY-307

TRADITIONAL TALES
from
AFRICA

Vic Parker

Based on myths and legends retold by
Philip Ardagh

Illustrated by
Georgia Peters

Thameside Press

Distributed in the United States by
Smart Apple Media
1980 Lookout Drive
North Mankato, MN 56003

Editor: Stephanie Turnbull
Designer: Zoë Quayle
Educational consultant: Margaret Bellwood

Library of Congress Cataloging-in-Publication Data

Parker, Vic.
Africa / written by Vic Parker.
p. cm. -- (Traditional tales from around the world)
Includes index.
Contents: African tales -- In the beginning -- The race -- Kigbo and the bush spirits -- The water god's challenge -- The old widow woman's children -- The lion man -- The battle with death.
ISBN 1-930643-35-7
1. Tales--Africa. [1. Folklore--Africa.] I. Title.

PZ8.1.P2234 Af 2001
398.2'096--dc21

2001027179

Printed in Hong Kong

9 8 7 6 5 4 3 2 1

Contents

AFRICAN TALES

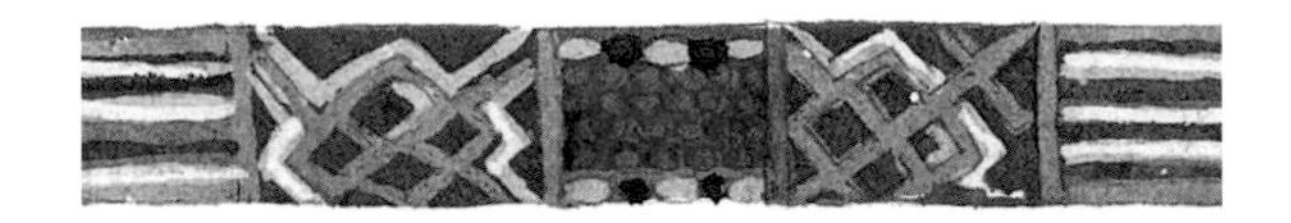

Africa is an enormous place. It is not just one country, it is a whole group of countries called a continent. Africa makes up nearly a quarter of all the land on Earth.

People have lived in Africa for thousands and thousands of years. Because Africa is so huge, people from different parts of the continent have their own languages, customs, religious beliefs, and favorite stories. These have spread all over the world, mainly because of the slave trade. This was when white people took hundreds of Africans to North America and the Caribbean islands and forced them to work on farms. The Africans struggled for freedom for many years.

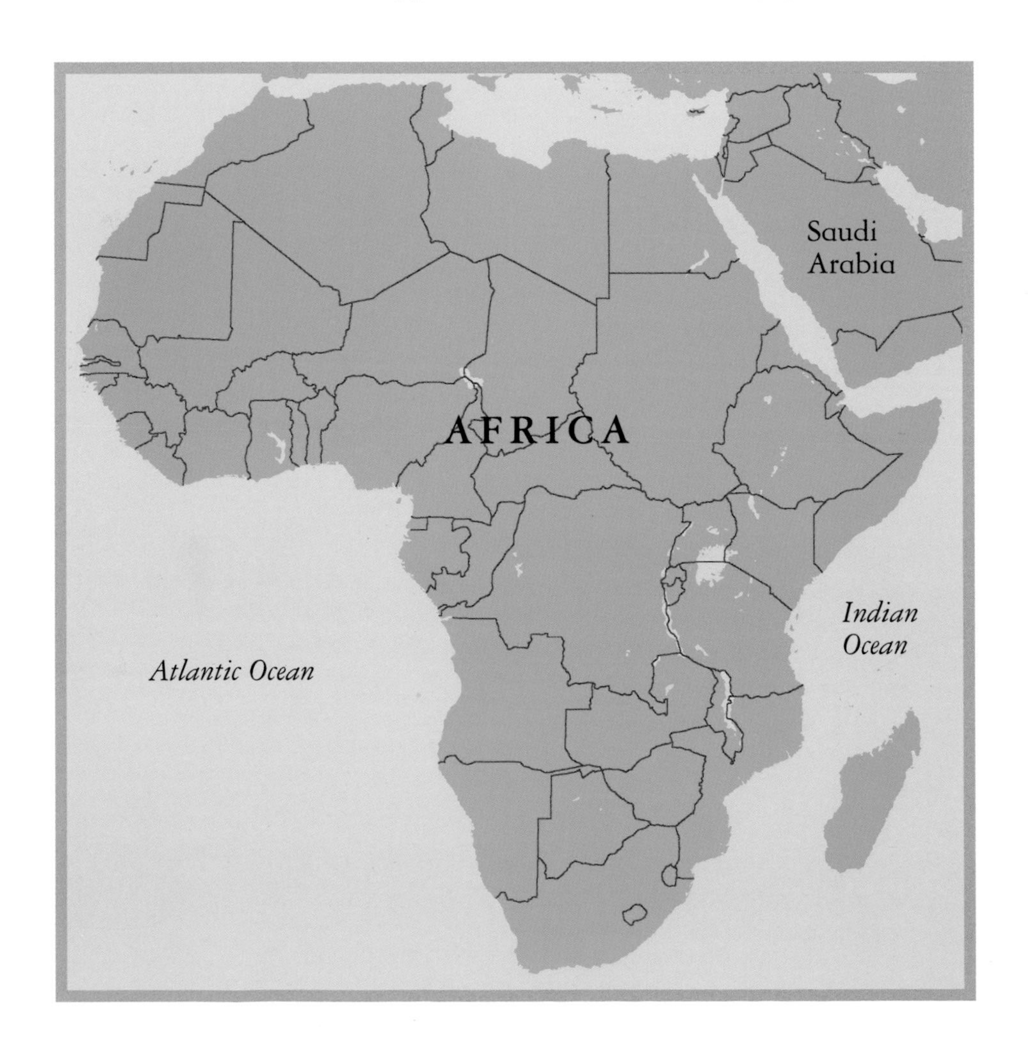

Much of Africa is covered by the world's largest desert, the Sahara. In other parts of Africa there is wide, thick jungle. Some African land is wild and difficult to farm. These areas are called the bush.

Over the years Africans have made up thousands of fantastic stories about the creatures who live in these places, such as the sly rats of the desert, the mischievous monkeys of the jungle, and the lazy hippos of the plains. For hundreds of years, people have thought that gods and spirits lived in the bush, so there are many wonderful stories about them, too.

In this book you can read exciting new versions of these tales, taken from many different peoples and cultures within the huge continent of Africa.

This painted wooden mask was made in Nigeria. Masks are worn in special ceremonies to contact spirits.

In the Beginning

In the beginning, the creator god decided to make the world. He took a big lump of clay and molded it into a smooth, round pot. He baked the pot in a huge oven, then he wrapped it in shining, red copper and set it in the sky. The creator god smiled.

"You are my Sun," he said.

The creator god was so pleased with the Sun that he made another pot. This one was smaller and he wrapped it in pale brass. The creator put the gleaming pot at the other end of the sky, far away from the Sun.

"You are my Moon," he said.

The creator god stood back and admired his work.

Hmmm, he thought. *The heavens are now very beautiful, but they need something else.*

He reached out and snapped off a bit of the Sun. He smashed it into a million pieces and scattered the fragments across the sky.

"Stars," he announced. "Perfect."

Next the creator god shaped another giant lump of clay into a ball, which he called the Earth.

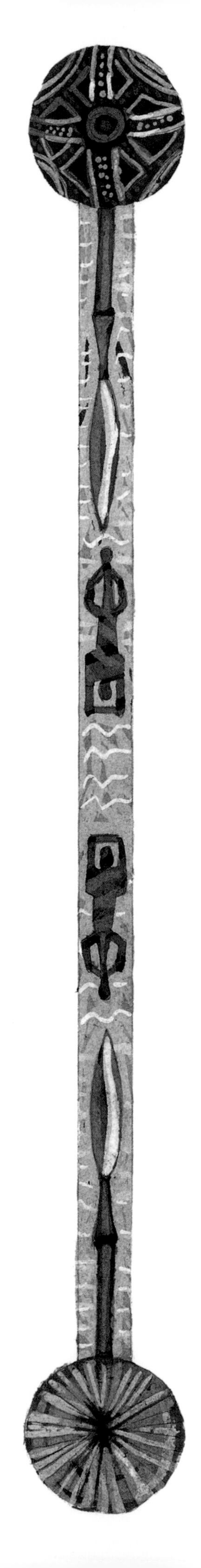

"You will be my wife," he told the Earth and sent down the very first shower of rain on it. To the creator god's joy, twins grew from the wet soil. He called his children Water and Light, and they joined him in the heavens.

Water and Light saw that their mother Earth was naked and bare. They hurried to make grass and plants grow into a robe to cover her.

Meanwhile, the creator god shaped more clay into the first man and woman. He breathed life into them and set them on the Earth. The creator god was delighted when the woman gave birth to eight children.

"What interesting creatures these humans are!" smiled Light. "Why don't you make some more?"

The creator god thought this was a good suggestion. He took some brilliant sunlight and made people with shining, black skins. He then took some gleaming moonlight and made people with pale, white skins.

"Well done!" said Water. "They are all wonderful."

The creator god sat and talked with Water and Light as they made a skirt of flowers and trees for their mother Earth. The braiding and weaving of their hands created a breeze that blew their words far away.

Down on Earth, humans heard these strange sounds. They understood them and began speaking to each other.

Soon the humans realized that there were words for things they had never seen.

"We know the meaning of words such as *mountain* and *river*," the people said to each other, "but what are words such as *dog*, *giraffe*, *whale* and *parrot*?"

One clever woman figured it out.

"If these things aren't down here with us, they must live up in the heavens with the creator god," she cried. "He must want to keep them for himself!"

"Then we'll have to go up there and steal them!" whispered a man.

The humans built a hollow wooden pyramid, big enough to contain all the things the creator god had kept for himself. They used a strong rope to drag the pyramid to the top of the highest mountain. A group of humans climbed up the pyramid, through the clouds, and found themselves in the heavens.

The people could hardly believe the wonderful things they found there. All around were brightly colored furry things and feathered things and scaly things. Things were scampering and fluttering and swimming. Things were squeaking and squawking and snorting. The amazed humans finally understood the meaning of the words *animals*, *birds*, *fish*, and *insects*.

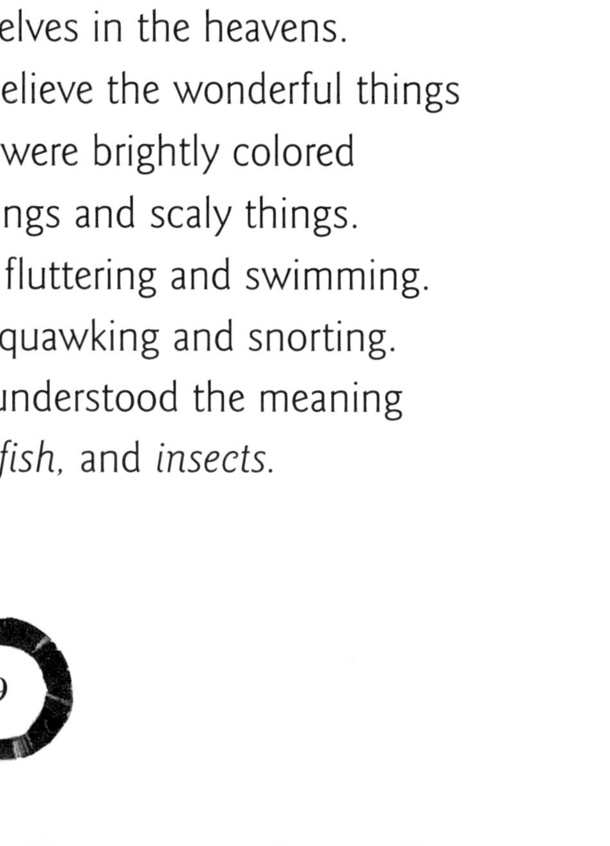

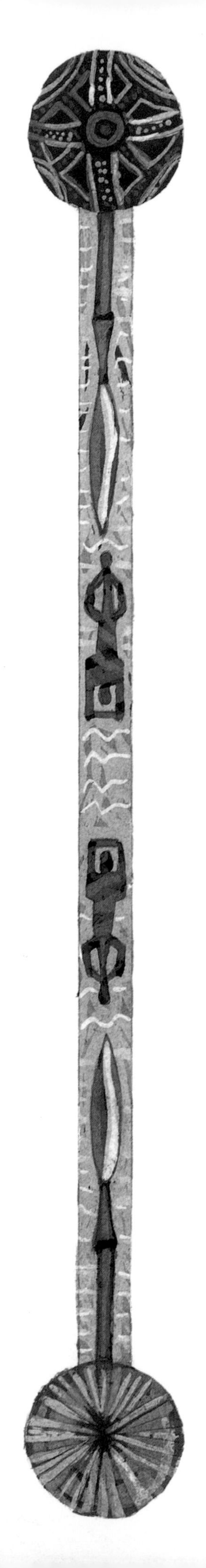

"They're so beautiful!" the people cried. "How clever the creator god is! We won't steal *all* his creatures. We'll just take one male and one female of each type."

Quickly, the humans packed the pyramid with pairs of animals. The largest were wedged in at the bottom. The smallest were jammed in at the top. When the last creature had been squeezed inside and the huge doors bolted shut, the pyramid was much heavier than anyone had imagined. It was much too heavy to be lowered back down with the rope. There was only one other way to return to Earth—down the rainbow.

With their hearts beating fast, the people made sure that one end of the rope was tied tightly to the pyramid. They looped the other end around the Sun. Slowly, they began to lower the pyramid down the rainbow bridge....

Way below, the men and women who had been left on Earth caught sight of the giant pyramid sliding down the rainbow. They began to cheer, but suddenly the sky thundered with an ear-splitting CRACK! and their shouts of excitement turned to cries of terror. The pyramid was hurtling toward them, and at the other end of the rope was a broken piece of the Sun! The people fled for cover as the burning fragment flew into a bush. It burst into a blaze of orange flames.

At first the people were terrified—they had never seen fire before. But once they recovered from the shock, they were very pleased.

"It is another gift from the creator god!" they yelled. "It gives heat and light! Imagine what we can do with it!"

Finally, everyone rushed to open the doors of the pyramid. The animals, fish, birds, and insects inside were unharmed. The humans gasped with joy as the creatures streamed out into their new home.

And that is how humans came to share the Earth with all sorts of animals. The creator god saw that his creatures were happy there, so he allowed them to stay.

The Race

The old king was very tired. Ruling was hard work, and he had done it for many long years. The old king made up his mind—enough was enough. He deserved a rest. It was time to hand over his crown to one of his sons, Prince Lizard or Prince Frog.

But which one should be the new king? Prince Lizard was handsome and strong. He was also a fast mover and did everything quickly. Prince Frog was slower, but he was also more thoughtful. The king sighed and shook his head. He loved both sons equally, and he couldn't decide between them. Also, he couldn't bear to upset one of them by not picking him. The old king shut his eyes and thought for a while....

That was it! The old king's eyes opened wide as a wise idea popped into his head. He wouldn't choose either of his sons—he would make them decide for themselves.

The old king called for his trusted chief minister and whispered his clever plan into the minister's ear. The chief minister nodded and smiled, then he hurried away to find the royal brothers.

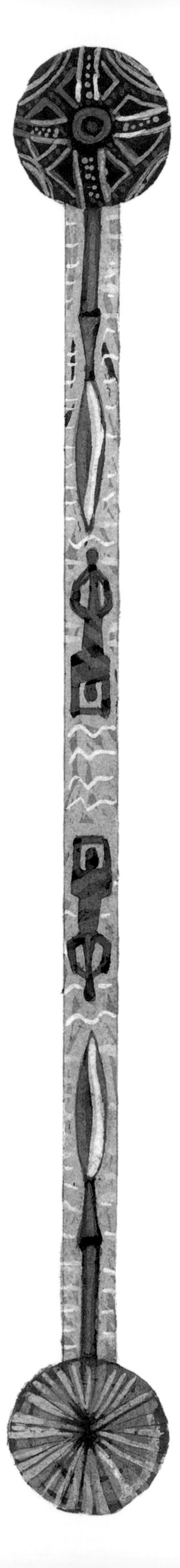

The chief minister searched for a long time and eventually came across the two princes at a rocky pool. Prince Frog sat half in and half out of the water, under a shady leaf. He liked to be cool and damp. If he got too hot, it made him ill. Prince Lizard sat out in the open, in the full heat of the noonday sun. His dry, scaly skin was baking nicely, just as he liked it. As usual, Lizard was boasting about what a good king he'd be one day. As usual, Frog was listening carefully and quietly.

"Good afternoon, your highnesses," the chief minister greeted the princes. "I come with an important message from his majesty, your father. He summons both of you to the palace immediately. Whoever gets there first will be the next king."

Prince Lizard cackled with delight. He knew that he was the speediest by far.

"Don't worry," he teased his brother. "If we've all gone to bed by the time you arrive, I'll tell them to keep the palace gates open for you." With that he slithered away across the ground and slipped out of sight.

Prince Frog sat and watched him go.

"It's true," he said to himself slowly and thoughtfully. "My brother Lizard is much faster than I am. Besides, I can't go out in the blazing sun or I will shrivel up and die."

Prince Frog shot out his tongue and swallowed a fly. "I will have to try some other way," he decided.

Prince Frog hopped through the shady undergrowth until he reached a magic tree. Gently, he broke off a twig and ground it into powder. Carefully, he blew the powder into the wind. Loudly, he croaked some magic words. The skies suddenly grew darker, then . . . splosh! A large drop of rain landed on Prince Frog's nose. Splish! There was another, on the ground. Splash! Splash! Splash! The rain began to come thick and fast. Prince Frog looked up at the black clouds and grinned a wide grin. His spell had worked! Steadily, he hopped away through the puddles on his way to the palace.

Prince Lizard was very nearly at the palace when the downpour began. He hated getting wet, and he hurried to take cover under a nearby rock.

It won't matter if I shelter here for a while, he thought to himself. *Frog will never catch up!*

He made himself comfortable and yawned. It was nice and dry under the rock and he was a little tired after all that running.... In a few seconds, he was fast asleep.

When Prince Lizard woke, the drumming of the rain had stopped. He poked his nose out from under the rock and felt warm sunshine beating down.

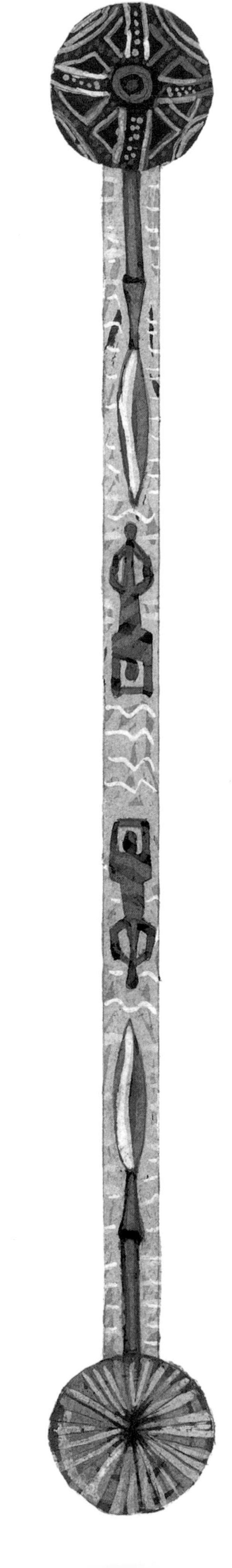

"Splendid!" he said to himself. He shot out from under the rock and set off once again.

It wasn't long before Prince Lizard saw the magnificent royal palace in front of him.

"Just think!" he said to himself gleefully. "Soon, all this will be mine!" Tears of pride came to his eyes as he heard the royal heralds trumpeting a fanfare to welcome him. Prince Lizard slowed to a dignified walk and the huge palace gates began to swing open to let him in.

Horror of horrors! It wasn't his father, the old king, who came out to greet him—but his brother! Prince Lizard's jaw dropped open.

"Prince Frog!" he squeaked. "How . . . but . . . what . . . " he began to stutter.

"Hello, Lizard," said Frog. "What kept you?"

Frog's magic rain shower had lasted long enough for him to catch up with Lizard—and then to overtake him.

"By the way, I'm not *Prince* Frog now," Frog continued, "I'm *King*." And there was nothing Lizard could do or say to argue with that!

So now you know that when you hear frogs croaking, you should take your umbrella out with you. They are saying the magic words that bring the rain....

Kigbo and the Bush Spirits

Kigbo was the sort of person who always had to do things his own way. No one knew where he got his determined ideas from, because his parents were quiet, simple people. Perhaps it had something to do with his name, for "Kigbo" means "stubborn man."

Eventually Kigbo got married and moved out of his parents' house. His father decided to make a suggestion to his stubborn son.

"Kigbo, it is time for you to stop working on my land," he said. "Now that you have a wife to look after, you need a farm of your own. Why don't we clear some land at the edge of the village, so you can have your own field?"

But Kigbo had other ideas. "That's little more than waste ground!" he scoffed. "Besides, it's much too small. I'm going to farm an area of the bush instead."

"The bush?" Kigbo's father gasped. "You must be mad! The bush is wild and dangerous land, and it's a long way from the village. What's more, the bush is full of spirits!"

"Nothing you can say will make me change my mind," announced Kigbo, so that was that.

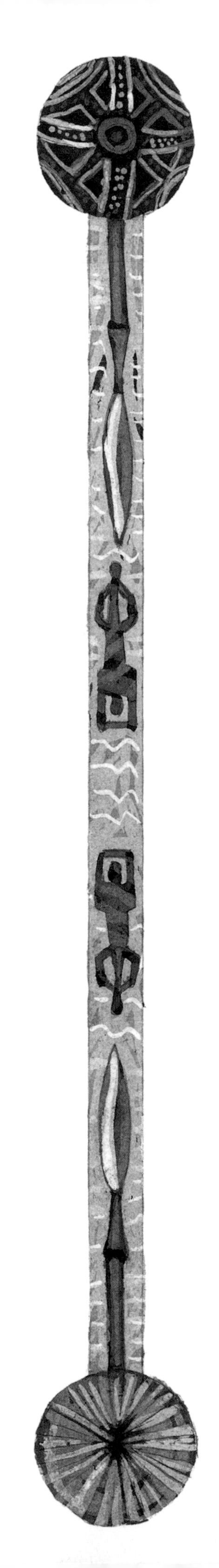

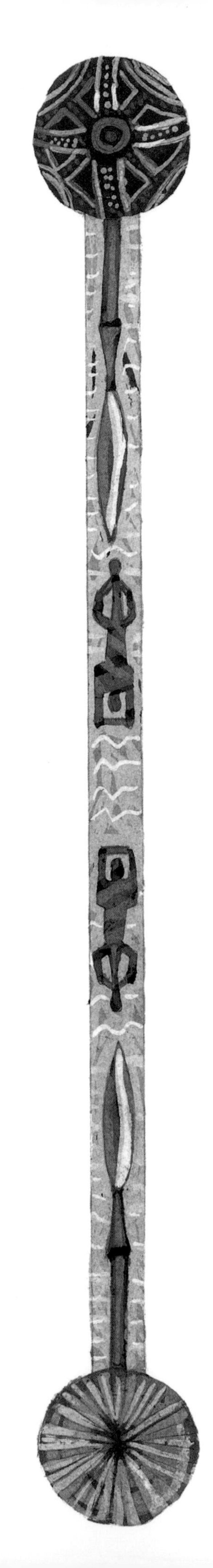

The next day Kigbo marched into the bush. The grass and leaves and bushes and vines grew thick and wild and as high as his head. He took his ax and began to hack away with all his might.

WHOOSH! Suddenly a group of bush spirits appeared out of nowhere.

"We are the bush spirits, and this is our land," the spirits said together. "We do what you do." They started clearing the bush in a blur of speed.

In next to no time, a huge area of undergrowth was cleared. Kigbo was delighted! Without a word of thanks to the bush spirits, he hurried home.

"My field is much larger than our neighbors' plots," Kigbo said happily to his wife.

Early the next morning, Kigbo returned to his field. The next job was to get the soil ready for planting. No sooner had Kigbo stuck his spade into the earth than WHOOSH—the bush spirits appeared again.

"We are the bush spirits, and this is our land," they chanted again. "We do what you do."

Kigbo couldn't believe his luck. With the magical help of the bush spirits, the whole field was dug over by the end of the day. Without a word of goodbye to the spirits, Kigbo strolled home.

“All our neighbors have to sweat for a week to dig their fields, but I have dug mine in one day!” Kigbo boasted to his wife.

Next day, Kigbo went to his field with a sack of seeds. He made a hole in the soil, put in a seed, patted some earth on top, and WHOOSH—the bush spirits appeared.

“We are the bush spirits, and this is our land,” they sang. “We do what you do.”

In an instant, the sack of seeds was empty, and Kigbo's crops were planted. *Easy as pie*, Kigbo thought, as he turned his back on the bush spirits and trotted home.

“Now all we have to do is wait,” he told his wife smugly.

Several weeks later, Kigbo noticed that his neighbors' fields were sprouting tiny, green shoots. Quickly, he hurried into the bush to check his field.

When Kigbo returned, his eyes were shining.

“Dear wife,” he laughed. “I was right all along! I have twice as many crops as anyone else, and they have already grown twice as high! In the morning, I will take you to see my fantastic field for yourself.”

That night, Kigbo's wife was so excited that she couldn't sleep. As the sun began to rise, she couldn't wait any longer. *Kigbo can catch up later*, she thought. She tied her baby to her back and headed into the bush.

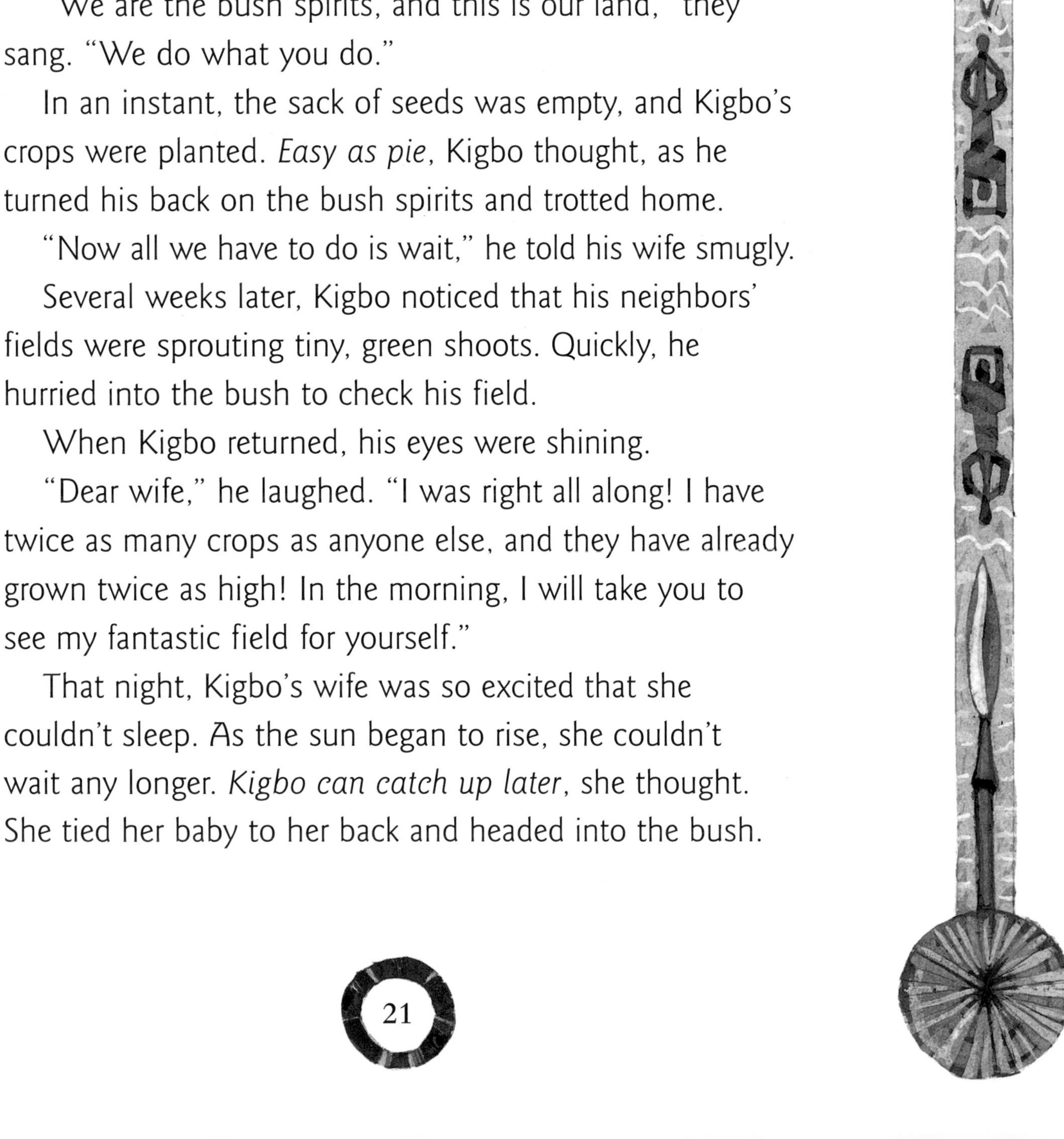

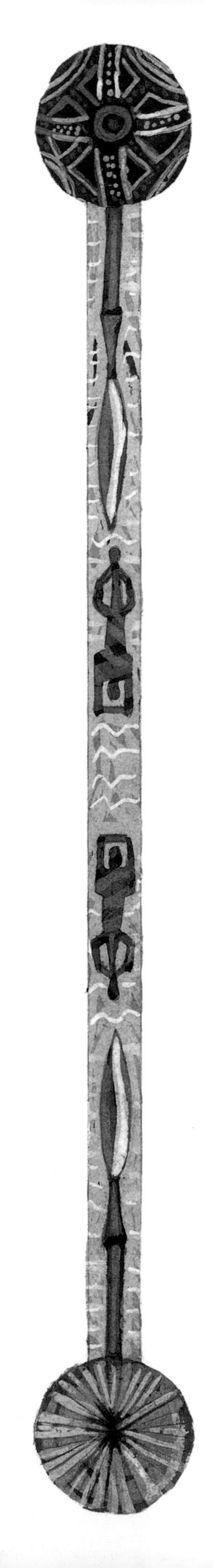

Kigbo's wife was overjoyed to find that the field was just as her husband had said. However, their tiny son was hungry after the long journey and wouldn't stop crying.

"There, there," soothed Kigbo's wife and broke off a stalk of grain to feed the little boy.

WHOOSH—the bush spirits appeared out of nowhere.

"We are the bush spirits, and this is our land," they yelled at Kigbo's terrified wife. "We do what you do!"

In a matter of seconds, all the grain was stripped off the plants and eaten.

At that very moment, Kigbo himself arrived.

"Please don't be angry with me!" his sobbing wife begged. 'I snapped off a stalk of grain for our son and all these terrible bush spirits appeared and did the same."

"Stupid child!" the furious Kigbo bellowed. He grabbed his little boy and began shaking him violently.

"We are the bush spirits, and this is our land," the spirits roared. "We do what you do!"

Before Kigbo could stop them, they seized his baby son and started shaking him.

"This is all your fault, you foolish woman!" yelled Kigbo. He began slapping his poor wife as hard as he could.

"We are the bush spirits, and this is our land," shrieked the bush spirits. "We do what you do!"

They rushed at Kigbo's wife, and she disappeared under their blows. Kigbo clapped his hands to his head in despair—and the spirits turned on him and began to beat him to the ground.

No one is really sure what finally happened to Kigbo, his wife, and his child. Some people say that the bush spirits killed them. Other people say that they managed to escape and that Kigbo was a changed person from that moment on. Whatever happened, one thing is certain: from that day to this, people with common sense have kept far away from the bush.

The Water God's Challenge

Olokun was the great god of water. He lived deep down in the sea in a magical palace, and he owned a mighty river that filled all the oceans of the world.

Olokun was a good and kind god, and he enjoyed making humans happy. It was Olokun who sent babies into the world, bringing great joy to people. He also gave humans many precious possessions. His greatest gifts were the lakes, rivers, and waterholes that brought life to Africa. It was thanks to Olokun that people had wells to drink from, rivers to wash in, and lakes to fish in. It was thanks to Olokun that crops, plants, and trees grew tall and green in the burning sun. It was thanks to Olokun that animals filled the plains and birds soared in the skies.

The men and women of Nigeria loved Olokun and worshiped him as their favorite god. They built him amazing temples and decorated them with expensive materials and delicately carved figures. People had statues of Olokun in their houses and prayed to the mighty god every day.

All this worshiping made Olokun feel very important.

So important, in fact, that he became very big-headed.

I shouldn't just be the god of water, Olokun began to think. *I should really be the chief god!*

The thought niggled away at Olokun until one day he exploded at his servant, "What can the chief god do for humans that I can't?"

"Um . . . I don't know!" the startled servant spluttered.

"Exactly!" roared the water god. "That's why I'm sending you to the chief god with a message. Tell him that I challenge him for his title of chief god!"

The servant gulped.

"Yes, my lord," he squeaked nervously. He dashed away to the chief god's palace, panicking all the way. Surely the chief god would be furious at such a bold message!

When the servant was shown into the chief god's magnificent chamber, his teeth were chattering and his knees were knocking with fear. He bowed low before the chief god's enormous throne.

"Y-y-your m-m-majesty...." the servant stuttered. "Y-y-your r-r-royal h-h-highness...."

"Enough!" the chief god commanded. "I can read the thoughts of all creatures, and I know why you have come."

The servant shut his eyes tightly and waited to be sent to the dungeons.

"Tell your master that I accept his challenge."

The stunned servant couldn't believe his ears.

"Of course, I am much too busy to meet Olokun myself," the chief god continued, with a secret smile. "I will send a messenger instead."

The servant scurried backwards out of the room, bowing all the way, and ran to Olokun with the news.

At first, the water god wasn't pleased at all.

"A messenger?" Olokun thundered. "I challenge the chief god and he sends a *messenger*?"

The servant thought quickly. "Perhaps the chief god is afraid to face you himself, my lord," he suggested.

"You must be right!" Olokun crowed. "I'll soon show this nobody of a messenger exactly what he is up against."

Olokun barked orders, and hundreds of servants sprang into action, dashing here, there, and everywhere. By the time a fanfare announced the arrival of the chief god's messenger, Olokun's underwater palace sparkled and glittered. Coral tables were set with delicious food. Beautiful music rippled through every room, and the floors shone with a million colorful shells.

Finally, the water god himself strode into his throne room. He was dressed splendidly in amazing robes that swirled and billowed like the waves of the ocean.

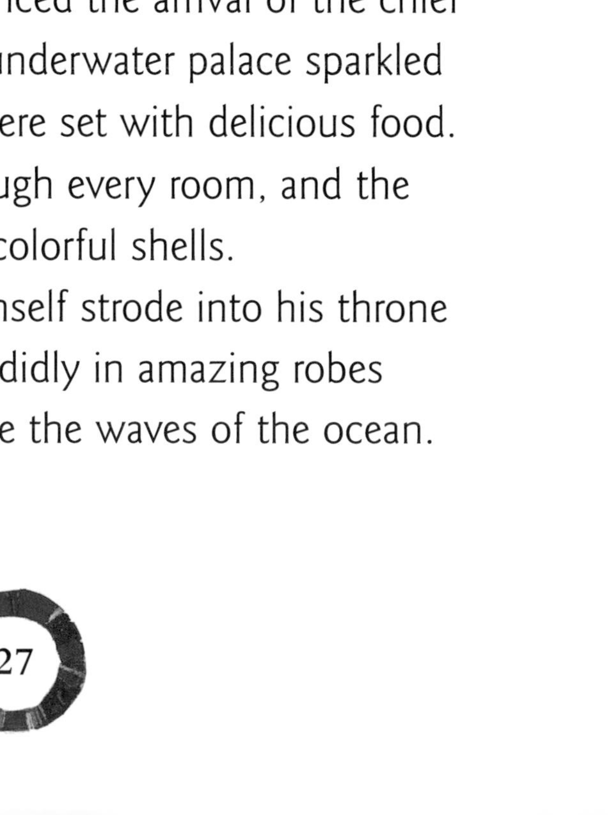

The moment Olokun caught sight of the messenger, he stopped dead in his tracks. The messenger was wearing the same clothes as he was!

"Will you excuse me for a minute?" Olokun muttered. "I really must change out of these old rags."

The water god hurried back to his dressing room, his face red with embarrassment.

It wasn't long before Olokun was back. This time, he was wearing robes that clung around him and shimmered like sea mist. Yet no sooner had Olokun laid eyes on the messenger than he turned and headed out again.

"Do forgive me!" he shouted over his shoulder. "I have spotted a speck of dirt on my robes. Allow me to change." Somehow, the messenger's clothes again matched Olokun's outfit!

When Olokun entered the throne room for the third time, everyone gasped. The water god was dressed in the very best clothes he owned. They were so rich and fine he had never even worn them before. Olokun had been saving them for when he became the new chief god. As he walked, the robes rippled and changed from the colors of sunrise, to sunset, to starry midnight. They rustled and swished with the secret songs of ancient sea creatures. No one had ever seen anything so beautiful.

Imagine Olokun's horror when he saw that the messenger had changed his clothes, too. Once again they were both wearing exactly the same robes!

Olokun realized he was beaten. He bowed his head in shame.

"Go back to the chief god," he whispered. "Give him my respects and tell him I have learned my lesson. I cannot compete with the chief god's messenger, let alone the chief god himself."

The water god never found out that the chief god's messenger was really a chameleon—an animal that changes its colors to match its surroundings. Olokun had been tricked by nature itself.

The Old Widow Woman's Children

There was once an old widow woman who lived all alone. She had once been a beautiful young girl and had married a strong, handsome man. They had been very happy together, but the man had died early, leaving the woman heartbroken. She had sworn never to marry again, and so she had never had any children.

The other old people in the village had families to carry their water, fetch their firewood, and help with the dusting and sweeping. The old widow woman had no one. Every day she shuffled around her house, bent and hunched over. Trying to keep her home tidy made her bones ache. Worrying about money made her head ache. Eating every meal alone made her heart ache.

The old widow woman did have one joy in life. She had planted a little garden in the shade of her neighbor's banana trees. There, she grew all sorts of beautiful flowers and tasty vegetables and juicy fruits. She cared for her plants as well as she could with her gnarled fingers, and she loved to see them grow. The old widow woman's favorite plants were big, round vegetables called gourds.

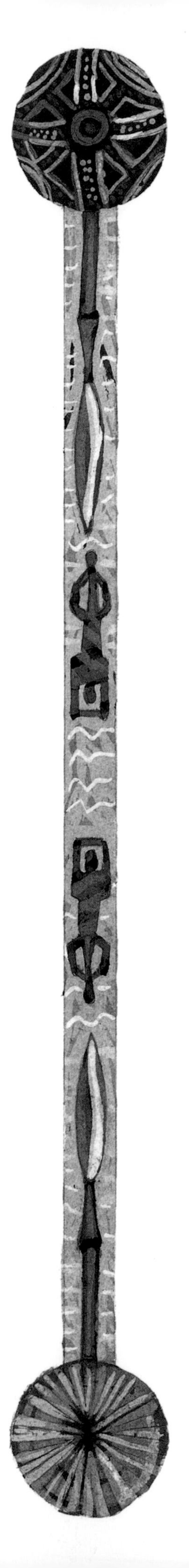

Each day she watered her shiny, plump gourds. She weeded them and shooed wild animals away. Whenever a gourd was ripe, the old widow woman pulled it gently off its stem. She carried it indoors and left it to dry out. When the skin was hard and smooth, she made the gourd into a bowl and sold it at the market. The money she made was just enough to buy food.

On the mountain behind the old widow woman's house lived a powerful spirit. One day the spirit looked down on the old widow woman and remembered how she had once been happily married. The spirit thought of how the old widow woman prayed to him faithfully every day of her life. The spirit's heart melted. He would take pity on her. He would give her the children she longed for.

Next morning, the old widow woman noticed that four gourds in her garden were ready for picking. She managed to heave three of them high into the rafters of her house to dry out. The fourth gourd was so fat and heavy that the old widow woman could hardly lift it. She managed to drag it into the house and left it sitting by the fire. Then she hurried off to market.

While the old widow woman was out, the mountain spirit sent a messenger creeping into the locked house.

The messenger softly touched each gourd, then vanished as mysteriously as he had arrived.

One by one, the four large gourds turned into sleeping children. They opened their eyes and yawned and stretched. They looked at each other in delight and began to giggle. The child who sat by the fire was big and plump and strong. He lifted the three little children down from the rafters, then sat back and watched as his brothers ran all over the old woman's house, busily cleaning and tidying, washing and cooking.

Soon, a large pile of firewood was stacked in the corner. A fire blazed in the hearth. A big pot of soup cooked over the flames. All the bowls were washed. The water jar was full to the brim. The floor was swept.

Just as the eldest brother was lifting the first, small child back into the rafters, the old widow woman returned from the market. Her mouth dropped open in surprise and joy as she realized where these four children had come from and what they had done to her house.

"Stop! Stop!" she cried. "Please don't turn into gourds again! Thank you for helping me like this. Stay and let me look after you, just as you are looking after me. Stay and be my children."

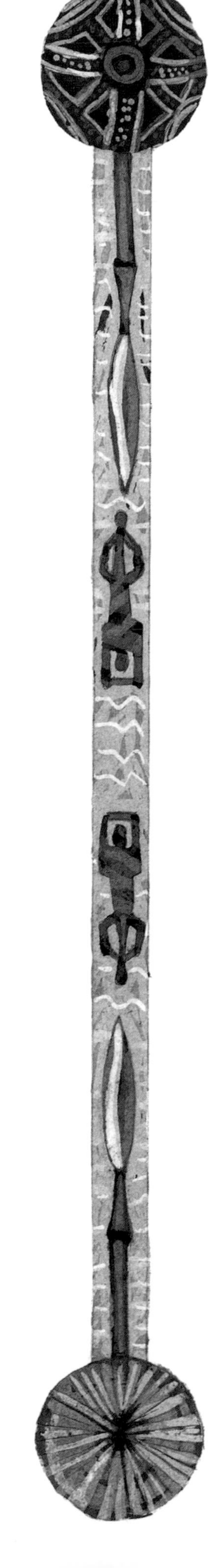

The old widow woman never questioned where her magical children had come from. She was much too happy to ask questions! Every day, the children's laughter filled the old widow woman's house as they kept her company and helped her with the household chores.

The children worked in the old widow woman's little garden, too. They grew more flowers, fruit, and vegetables than ever before. The old widow woman had so many gourds that she didn't know where to store them all. Soon she had enough money to buy her neighbor's banana trees. Later she bought her neighbor's land. Next she bought a herd of goats. Finally she became a very rich farmer, and all her worries were over. The rich old widow completely forgot what it was like to be lonely and poor and unloved.

One day, the rich old widow was carrying a huge pot of stew when she tripped over the biggest child, who was sitting in his usual place by the fire. No one was hurt, but the stew spilled everywhere. The rich old widow was so annoyed that she lost her temper.

"You stupid boy, lazing in front of the fire!" she yelled angrily. "I don't know why I bother to look after you four anymore. I could pay real servants to work for me now. After all, you're only GOURDS!"

As the final word passed her lips, the eldest boy turned back into a gourd. In horror the rich old widow looked at the other children. They too had turned back into gourds.

At once, the rich old widow deeply regretted her hasty words. But no matter how much she wailed and begged, the children never returned. No matter how many other gourds she grew, they never turned into new children. For the rest of the rich old widow's days, her house was empty, quiet, and still.

The Lion Man

There were once three herdsmen who owned a large herd of cattle. They looked after their animals well. Every day, they walked the cattle to new grasslands, to graze under the blazing sun. Every night, they slept with the cattle under the stars, keeping guard against thieves. Every year, they had many fat animals to sell at market.

One night, a huge lion came stalking the cattle. The herdsmen huddled together in the darkness and trembled at the terrifying roars. In the morning, one of their best cows was missing. The next night, the lion stole another cow. The following night, yet another cow was taken.

"What are we going to do?" the herdsmen panicked. "If we try to fight the lion, we will surely be killed. But if we don't do something, we'll soon have no herd left!"

Later that day, a medicine man came calling from a nearby village.

"I know there's a savage beast roaming around these parts," the medicine man explained, "and I thought you might need some help. I have magic that will keep the lion away from you and your herd for one month."

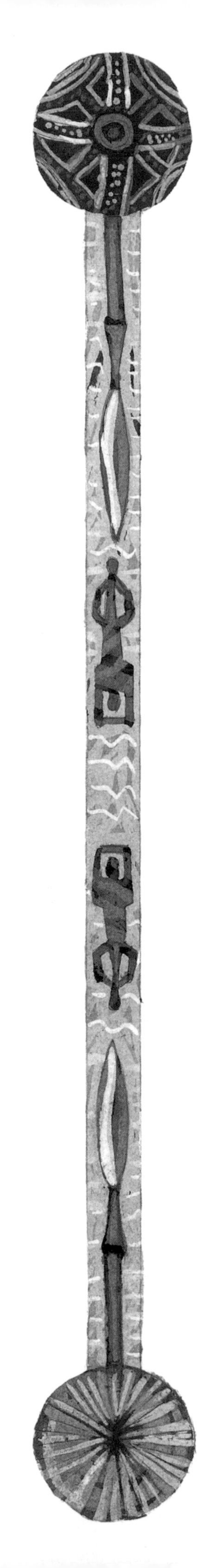

The herdsmen were overjoyed, but their faces soon fell when they heard the price.

"It is a very expensive spell," the medicine man warned. "It will cost you the biggest, fattest cow in your herd."

The cattle herders had no choice. If they didn't give the medicine man their prize cow, the lion would eat it anyway! The herdsmen nodded their agreement.

The medicine man dressed in his best robes and put on special face paint. He took out his charms and made up his potions. He sprinkled his powerful spell around the herd and said his magic words. It was done. The medicine man led away the prize cow without a word.

Back in his own village, the medicine man took the cow into his home. That night the villagers could hear the sound of a wild beast tearing apart an animal and crunching its bones, but they had no idea where the sound was coming from.

Meanwhile, the herdsmen had a peaceful night. The lion was nowhere to be seen. The medicine man's magic had worked!

The herd was safe for a month, just as the medicine man had said. Then the lion struck again. This time it was in broad daylight. One of the herdsmen ran bravely toward the beast, shouting angrily and waving his spear.

The lion ignored him. He was huge and wild and fearless. He sank his sharp teeth and claws into the neck of the largest cow and dragged it into the bush. By the time the herdsman reached the spot, the beast and his catch were gone.

There was nothing for the cattle herders to do but buy more expensive magic. This time, the herdsmen asked the medicine man to protect their cattle for *three* months.

"I can certainly do that," the medicine man nodded, "but three times the magic is three times the price."

"We can't give you any cattle to take away today because it is calving time," the herdsmen explained. "However, we promise that if you perform your magic, we will bring three cows to you as soon as we can."

"It must be three of your *best* cows," the medicine man reminded them.

The cattle herders watched solemnly as the medicine man worked his powerful spell. Once again, they breathed a deep sigh of relief.

Days passed . . . then weeks . . . then a month or two . . . and there was no sign of the lion. The herdsmen began to forget their fear.

"Let's move the herd without paying the medicine man," they finally agreed.

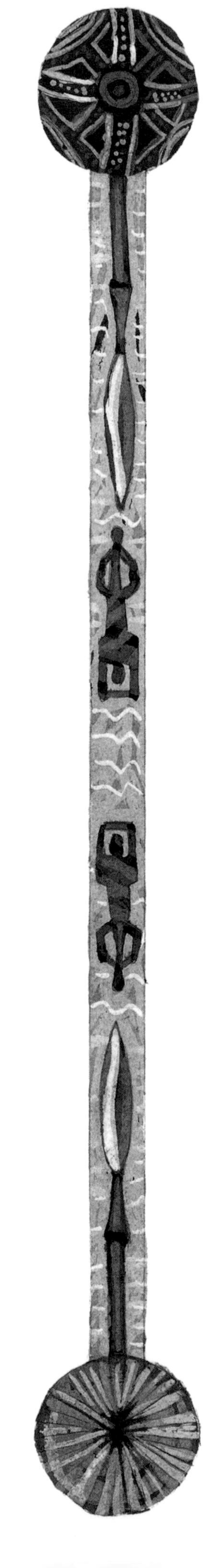

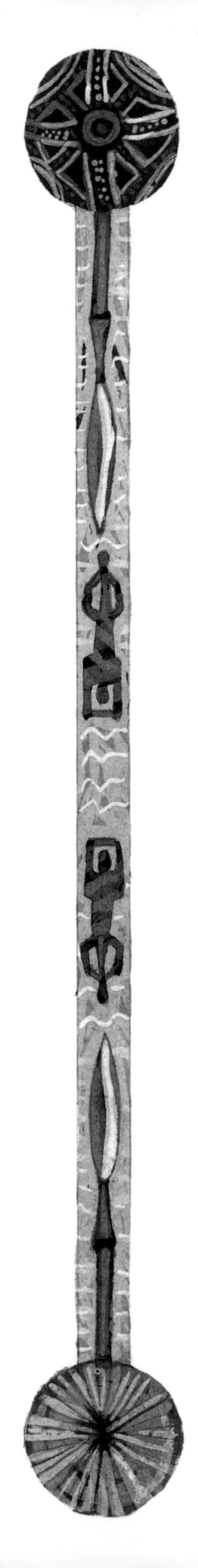

That very day, the three herdsmen packed their few belongings and rounded up the cattle. They crossed the river and headed far away into new fields.

It wasn't long before the medicine man heard that they had gone. He roared with fury and set off at once to find the cheating herdsmen. The raging medicine man followed the trail of hoofprints all the way to the river and found a ferryman to take him to the other side.

Little did the medicine man know that the ferryman was actually the river chief. He had magic powers of his own and could see things that other people couldn't see. The ferryman looked hard and saw that the medicine man wasn't at all what he seemed to be. His eyes were really golden. His teeth were really sharp and pointed. His skin rippled with fur just under the surface. His thick hair was really a shaggy mane. The ferryman could see that the medicine man was really the lion, disguised by magic!

Now, all lions have a habit of taking a midday nap when the sun is at its hottest. As soon as the boat reached the far riverbank, the medicine man found a shady tree and settled down for a snooze. He licked his lips hungrily as he dreamed of catching up with the herdsmen and pouncing on more of their tasty cattle!

But the medicine man never woke up again. While he was sleeping in his human form, the ferryman crept up and shot him dead with a magic arrow. As the medicine man's life left his body, he changed back into his true shape. There was a huge, wild beast lying dead at the ferryman's feet.

No one ever found out where the medicine man had disappeared to, and no one ever discovered what had happened to the lion. People in those parts are just glad that they have never been bothered by lions since.

THE BATTLE WITH DEATH

The man shaded his face with his hands and peered into the bright sky. The sun was so huge and hot that it dazzled him. The whole sky seemed to be on fire. The man couldn't see a single cloud. He hung his head in despair. There hadn't been a drop of rain for weeks now—no, months.

All around, the land was bare and cracked. There wasn't a blade of grass or a green leaf as far as the eye could see. Everything was dry and brown—except for heaps of bones that gleamed white in the dust. They were the bones of animals who had died of hunger and thirst.

The man sighed. He and his family and friends were hungry and thirsty too. Everyone had grown so thin that their clothes flapped loosely around them. Their lips were cracked, and when they licked them, their tongues were dry. All the drinking wells had dried up except one. No one knew how long that well would last. When the water ran out.... The man shuddered to think of what would happen to them.

As the man stared hopelessly into the distance, he noticed the dark figure of a person, a long way off. The figure was heading toward the village.

As the figure drew near, the man grew puzzled. The person didn't look like anyone he knew. The traveler was wrapped in a flowing cloak, but the man could tell that his arms and legs were muscular and strong. The traveler's eyes were hidden by a hood, but the man could see that his skin was healthy and glowing.

"You are welcome to our village," the man greeted the stranger. "You must have come from far away."

"I come from near and far," whispered the mysterious cloaked figure.

There was something about the stranger's voice that sent chills down the man's spine. Still, the man asked politely, "Did you see any rain along the way?"

"The lands I passed through were dry and bare," came the reply from deep within the hood.

Thoughts began to buzz through the man's brain like mosquitoes. "Have you seen much death?" he asked.

"Death was everywhere I went," the stranger said softly.

"What is your secret?" the man challenged, his heart racing. "Who are you and why are you so healthy?"

"You do not want to know," the stranger warned.

“I think I know already,” the man cried. “You *are* Death!”

The traveler threw off his hood. His eyes were lifeless and cold.

“Yes,” he hissed, “and in the end, everyone comes to know me.”

The man realized why Death had arrived in his village, and anger swelled up inside him.

“I am glad you have come to my village in human form,” he shouted. “You often creep up and take people by surprise. Well, my friends and I are brave and proud. We will be glad to look you in the face!”

Death was quiet for a moment. Then he murmured, “Are you really not afraid of me?”

“No!” yelled the man. “I’ll fight you anytime! In fact, I’ll fight you right here and now. I’ll fight you fair and square for my life and the life of everyone in the village!”

Death’s lips almost broke into a faint smile.

“Very well,” he said softly.

Before the man had a chance to prepare himself, Death sprang at him. The man fell into the dust with Death on top of him. He gasped for breath. He felt Death’s icy grip fasten tightly around his bones. The man thought about all the loved ones Death had already taken from him and all those who would die if he lost the wrestling match.

With a roar of rage, the man found new strength and threw Death to the ground. The pair rolled over and over and over, punching and kicking and clawing.

People from the village came hurrying out to cheer the man on. Even the sick and the dying begged to be carried out of their houses. Everyone wanted to watch the brave man who was fighting for their lives.

At the end of the long struggle the man stood bloody and exhausted, but it was Death who lay in the dirt, groaning.

"I am beaten," Death moaned, but then with one last effort he lashed out with a vicious blow. CRUNCH! The man felt his kneecap shatter into a thousand splinters of bone and flesh. He toppled over into the dust, and everything went black....

When the man came to he could hear the soft murmur of voices.

"Tsui'goab defeated Death," said one voice. "He saved his people."

"Yes," came another voice. "Now, with the gifts we have given him, Tsui'goab can give his people new life."

Who is this Tsui'goab? wondered the man. He opened his eyes and blinked. To his astonishment, he was lying high in the sky. Down below, he could see his village.

All of a sudden, the man understood. *He* was Tsui'goab. The words meant "wounded knee." He was now a god, and this was his new name!

Tsui'goab wondered what gifts he had been given. He stretched out his arms and watched in amazement as rain began to pour from his fingers. Down below, the villagers came running out of their houses, gazing up at the skies in disbelief. The rain soaked their clothes and washed over the cracked earth. Tsui'goab watched as the villagers began to dance for joy in the sudden downpour, and up in heaven, he smiled.

Index